Self-Esteem

Learn How To Conquer Your Fears, Boost Your Confidence, And Accept Who You Really Are

(A Self-Confidence Book For Adults: Boosting Your Self-Esteem And Building Your Confidence)

Sidney Friedman

TABLE OF CONTENT

Getting What You Want Out Of Life 1
Superior Capabilities In The Field Of Entrepreneurship 6
Powerful Connections To Both Animals And Plants 10
Psychology Of The Positive 13
A Guide To Overcoming Your Fears 19
A Piece Of Advice That Will Help You Get Motivated 27
The Language Of The Body And Its Physiology 43
Reorganization Of Thought Processes 49
Recognizing The Degree Of Self-Confidence You Possess 60
Goalsetting 69
How To Improve Your Self-Esteem And Stand Out Despite Being An Introvert 75
The Distinction Between Having Low Self-Confidence And Naturally Being An Introvert 81

Fear 90
Putting Your Objectives Down In Writing 97
A Value Structure That Is Consistent 105
Become The Aware Observer Of Your Own Thoughts. 112
Altering Feelings Through Changes In Behavior 117

Getting What You Want Out Of Life

You are gaining that self-confidence, which means that you are going to feel comfortable speaking up and letting the employer know that you are around and that you are a fantastic employee because of the progress you are making in this area. You are not going to have any problems accepting the credit that is rightfully yours due to the effort that you have put in. Your self-assured stride and posture are going to attract some attention as you come into the office, and you are going to be the center of it.

It is important that you recognize, before we get too further into boosting your self-esteem, that there is a balance between being exceedingly shy and being extremely overconfident. You want to be somewhere close to the center of the action. It is OK to recognize when you have accomplished something wonderful, and it is acceptable to take the acclaim that is rightfully yours. When someone walks around like a peacock and brags about how fantastic they are to anyone who would listen to them, it is tiresome and can sometimes even be considered disrespectful. That kind of behavior is known as arrogant. If you are arrogant, it signifies that you have gone too far and need to tone it down a bit. You will not gain any friends by arrogance, and in the end, it will cost you some friends along with any respect you have earned.

A crucial component of being successful is having faith in one's own abilities. If you don't start working on your self-confidence right away, you won't have a chance of doing anything you set out to do. Before you can ever achieve success, you need to convince yourself that you are capable of achieving it. When you tell yourself that you want an A on your term paper or a promotion, you might have a few moments of self-doubt, but deep down, you know that you are capable of achieving your goals and that you are good enough.

If you lack self-confidence, you won't even bother to try to achieve the goals you've set for yourself, and you probably won't even be able to establish any goals at all. You will realize that you are unable to escape the rut that you are in and that you are rapidly moving into a place of hopelessness as a result of your circumstance. On the other hand, doing nothing is a lot worse option than attempting anything and failing.

Why is it important to maintain a healthy level of self-confidence in order to be successful in achieving your goals?

You will have the guts to give it a shot, to embark on an adventure into the unknown, and you will succeed.

-You will have sufficient faith in yourself to take the next step toward achieving a goal.

You will have the passion and the drive that are need to achieve your goals.

You have the ability to refuse to participate in activities that do not interest you or that would waste your time.

Your self-assurance will help you overcome the fear that is holding you back.

You don't need to be afraid of the unknown in order to take advantage of interesting opportunities when they offer themselves to you.

Because of your self-assurance, you are able to create ambitious goals that will assist you in achieving fantastic achievements rather than setting modest goals that provide you with very little success.

You are capable of defending yourself diplomatically and commanding the respect you are due with panache.

Superior Capabilities In The Field Of Entrepreneurship

Entrepreneurs would do well to develop their intuitive faculties and improve their problem-solving skills; empaths make excellent businesspeople. They have a laser-like concentration on providing the very best outcomes for their customers, irrespective of the industry in which those customers operate. In addition, they are strongly motivated by the need to have independence and to get away from the poisonous, overpowering, and greedy settings of regular 9 to 5 jobs. This desire drives them.

Entrepreneurs with empathy are particularly skilled at conceiving of novel businesses that cater to the requirements of their customers in ways that larger corporations are more likely to entirely neglect. They frequently establish their own businesses, which are geared on bringing about some kind of social transformation or healing in today's world. Empaths frequently pursue careers as counselors, life and business coaches, alternative healers, artists, writers, and a variety of other professions. Empaths also frequently choose these types of careers. Fortunately, each of them may be approached as a business opportunity in and of itself. They are also ideal selections because they cater to the specific abilities and limitations of the empath, enabling the empath to shine as brightly as they possibly can while also allowing them to serve in the manner in which their soul requires them to shine.

If you are an empath and you are not currently on the route of becoming an entrepreneur, you may discover that commencing this life path brings you a great deal of joy and value. You have the potential to launch your life as an entrepreneur and achieve a high level of success in that endeavor because to the gifts and qualities you possess. The decision to pursue this line of work comes with a number of significant advantages. A few examples of these advantages are as follows:

When compared to having a job, having no employment gives you a significant increase in the amount of freedom and flexibility you have in your life.

You are in charge of determining your own work schedule as well as vacation time.

You do not have to put up with the exhausting and hazardous conditions that come with a typical 9 to 5 work.

You are free to collaborate with anybody you like, or you can opt to do all of your work online.

You have the option to work from home, where you have the ability to earn far more money than you would in a traditional job.

You have the opportunity to put your creative skills to good use.

Develop a sense of accomplishment and contentment in the work that you do.

It's possible that you'll have access to more travel opportunities.

When you remove yourself from toxic and negative work situations, you will notice an improvement in your general health and happiness.

A lot of people think that empathic entrepreneurship is going to be the most successful business model in the future. huge firms and corporations are often renowned for being reckless, rude, and brutal in their business dealings. As more and more people want to lead lives that are more socially conscious and responsible, many of them are avoiding doing business with huge businesses and organizations. These very same individuals are looking for business owners that are operating their own socially responsible companies in a manner that satisfies their requirements on a personal level in a true and authentic way. Because you are an empath, you already possess all of the skills necessary to serve in this capacity, which means that these individuals are looking for someone just like you and your abilities.

Powerful Connections To Both Animals And Plants

Empaths have a strong connection with both animals and plants, which is another one of their many strengths. You may already be familiar with animal empaths and plant empaths, and you may also be aware of the extraordinary abilities that these types of people possess when it comes to interacting with animals and plants. In a world in which very little regard has been shown to the environment and the people who inhabit it, this comes as a welcome and much-needed breath of fresh air. In today's modern world, many people rarely think about other people of their own species, let alone other species or living forms. You may have a powerful ability to relate to these living forms as an empath, and as a result, you may be able to save them from the harm caused by humans who have little to no experience with empathy in their lives.

It is thought that animals and plants are empathetic as well, which means that you can discover that animals and plants respond favorably to you as well. It's possible that you'll be able to bring animals into your life and have an unusual capacity to make plants flourish in a way that other people might have trouble accomplishing. This is due to the fact that they are perceptive and can tell when you are being charitable. Because of this, they will naturally trust you and will experience feelings of being safe, protected, and nourished while they are in your presence. They pick up on your enthusiasm, and they attribute their success in part to it.

Psychology Of The Positive

The United States is considered to be the birthplace of the positive psychology movement, which began in the 1960s and 1970s. The field of positive psychology, often known as PP, originated as a movement that applied the fundamentals of psychology to everyday life. This was done so that laypeople, who were not necessarily schooled in the intricacies of psychological theory, could comprehend the concepts and attempt to apply them to their own lives. Instead of merely attempting to keep people alive and ensure their survival, the goal of positive psychology is to help individuals thrive in all aspects of their lives. Do you notice a difference between the two? There is a mechanism within us that will help us live longer when all we are doing is living and surviving, and there is also an innate drive within us to continue living. However, in order for humans to genuinely grow, certain requirements of theirs must be satisfied.

This is what differentiates those who are only living from those who are thriving. When all you are doing is existing or surviving, your life may take on a particular appearance. It's possible that you're providing for your fundamental requirements as a person, such as having a place to sleep, food to eat, a job, and any number of other things that are essential to human existence. On the other hand, if you are thriving, you will have the opportunity to experience a more profound degree of life on this world. An someone who is flourishing has had meaningful life experiences. They are able to incorporate profoundly painful experiences with profoundly joyful and happy ones without losing themselves in either one. A person who is flourishing will have the ability to form connections with the individuals with whom they have expressed an interest in forming connections. They will come rather near to realizing their full potential as a human being. They will also have the ability to assist others in acquiring the skills and knowledge necessary to develop into a more self-actualized version of themselves. This blooming can be attributed to a few different locales. Self-expression, connection, meaningful relationships, and significance are some examples of these. A significant factor is meaningfulness.

People spend their entire lives looking for their life to have some sort of purpose. Finding and perceiving something meaningful is not something that we are always capable of doing. It is something that requires a lot of effort on our part most of the time. People are born into different circumstances; some are born into extreme poverty, others are born into the middle class, and yet others are born into the upper echelons of society. People who are already successful might have an easier job of it, but everyone has to figure out how to give their lives purpose.

Meaning is something that we must define for ourselves, and it can come from the tiniest things or the largest portions of our life. Meaning can come from everywhere in our lives. The goal of positive psychology is to help people discover the significance they seek in their life so that they can flourish.

Self-expression is a significant component of flourishing as well. If a person never allows themselves to communicate who they are or what they feel, they will discover that they are lacking in an important component of human functioning. In order for this to be done properly, people need to learn how to express themselves without resorting to judgment. One more thing that is necessary for human thriving is having meaningful relationships with other people. The majority of people need to develop their ability to connect with others in order to be successful. We were all born from the body of another human, and our ability to relate to people begins at this most fundamental level because of this fact. The only way for humans to mature is to learn from the experiences of other people; else, our species would perish. At this level, there is such a profound requirement for connection amongst people. In order for us to discover who we are and our role in the world, we have to start young and learn how to connect with our families or, at the very least, figure out what our families represent to us. A human life is not a human life if it is disconnected from others.

A Guide To Overcoming Your Fears

This is a significant question since there are so many various kinds of dread that a person can experience, and every person experiences them in a different way. Furthermore, the way in which a person feels fear is also unique to that person. In this section, we are going to focus on fears that are associated with one's level of self-confidence and self-esteem. Some examples of these fears are the fear of performing in front of others, the fear of being in unfamiliar settings, the fear of being rejected, and other similar fears.

Paying attention to your consciousness and where its emphasis is will be the first strategy we go through in this article for overcoming fear if you are a person who suffers from low levels of self-confidence or poor levels of self-esteem. If this describes you, keep reading! This means that at any given time, our conscious thoughts are focused on one or a couple of things, and most of the time we are oblivious to the fact that this is happening since it occurs so quickly and shifts so frequently. The important thing is to either pay attention to it or be aware of what our thoughts are primarily centered on. The first step in effecting any kind of change is just being aware of the problem, and that is precisely what our endeavor aims to accomplish. You are able to intervene in the automatic process of your thoughts and the processing of your thoughts when you become aware of your thoughts and where your focus is. This enables you to make adjustments before fear has the opportunity to take over. In the beginning, you are going to start by paying attention to your thoughts at arbitrary moments spread out throughout the day. This is so that you can grow used to observing your automatic thoughts as well as your shifts in consciousness. As soon as you begin to feel more at ease with doing this, you will be better able to do it in those times when your thoughts are racing, such as when you are afraid. If you pay attention to your thoughts when you are experiencing fear, you will be able to figure out what it is that is making you feel afraid in the first place. You won't have to make a decision about a circumstance based on the anxiety that's causing your mind to race away from you; instead, you'll be able to take the time to organize your ideas and come to a choice that's more well-informed. As was mentioned before, when fear takes control of your mind, it leads you to feel the fight or flight response. This response, which is purely focused on survival and does not allow any room for cognitive processing, reasoning, or assessing the pros and cons of a situation, prevents you from doing any of these things. I have included an illustration of what this looks like below for your reference.

Your body and mind automatically go straight to thoughts of terror when you see your ex-girlfriend in the metro station. Your body wants to either run away or approach her and get into a verbal argument with her.

In a normal situation, you would make a decision in this single second without even thinking about it, and the next thing you would know, your legs would be either carrying you over to her to fight or racing back up the stairs to go. However, what you are going to do instead is when you feel that feeling of fear coming over, you are going to take a deep breath and note that your mind is asking you to either fight or flee from the situation. This is something that you are going to do when you feel that feeling of fear taking over. The first thing to do is take note of this. When you bring an unconscious process into your waking awareness, you will have a greater degree of control over it.

You will then take a few moments to think about the situation and make a decision based on the information you have gathered rather of allowing your subconscious mind and your body to make the decision for you out of fear.

You are going to reflect about the last time you saw them, how the encounter went, how you feel about them now, and what you want to get out of this experience so that you can figure out how to handle the current circumstance. After you have done so and have taken a few deep breaths to calm yourself down, you will be able to make a decision regarding whether you will walk over to her and say hello or whether you will walk further down the platform in order to get on a different subway car than she is in order to avoid having to speak to her.

Observe how the options changed from "go and start a fight or run away" to "go and say hello or get on the subway at the other end" as the conversation progressed. There is no longer a choice between fighting and running away; rather, there are now two possibilities that require deliberate consideration. After giving it some more thought, I realized that there might be more than two choices available. If you just went through a particularly painful breakup, you might find it helpful to leave the metro station before the train departs and then return after it has passed. It's probably best if you just wave from a distance and let it go at that. You can come up with options for yourself by thinking about it for a few minutes, and then you can choose the best one deliberately based on your requirements and level of comfortability rather than out of a fear response. You can do this by thinking it through.

You may make it easier for yourself to become aware of what is happening in your mind during times of fear by practicing becoming aware of your thoughts and what is going on in your mind when you are on autopilot. This will allow you to intervene in the fight or flight response. In order to get better at this, you should strive to become aware of your thoughts more frequently during the day over a period of time, so that you can become familiar with the sensation of bringing your subconscious thoughts into your conscious mind.

A Piece Of Advice That Will Help You Get Motivated

Every one of you is driven by something, but that something is going to look different for everyone of you. There are straightforward activities that you can engage in that have the potential to motivate you, such as going shopping or simply having some spare time on your hands. No matter what it is that drives you, there are certain things that will keep you in a motivated mood even after the initial motivation has worn off.

There will be times, despite the many efforts you put in to succeed in life, when your motivation will seem to plummet over the edge of a cliff. These are quite common occurrences, and fortunately, there are straightforward solutions to the problems that they provide.

1) Creativity and fantasy

If you can imagine anything, you can make it happen. Someone once remarked that whether you believe you can do something or not, you are right in either case.

The human imagination is an inexhaustible source of information for us. It is what motivates people to think of new things that can make life better for themselves and others. It is also the beginning of the process of motivating others. Imagining how things will start, the excitement of a well-coordinated event, and the desired result are three things that are likely to fuel anyone's ambitions.

On the other hand, though, there is a single twist to this. It is important for us to steer clear of thinking bad ideas or having contradictory imaginations because they can have unfavorable consequences. A pessimistic imagination can only accomplish so much, and that is to sow seeds of doubt. It is impossible for it to be of any use to you, and it would in no way motivate us.

On the other hand, recognizing the significance of influence in appropriate amounts can be beneficial. Please don't push it to the point where it would undermine the entirety of the motivational plot that we have. Just by thinking positively and imagining something greater, we may lift our spirits and motivate ourselves to take action.

2) Make Being Motivated a Part of Your Routine

There is always the possibility that we could accomplish something truly remarkable right up until our very last breath. Even though we may have accomplished some of our objectives, this does not mean that our lives are finished and that we do not require any additional inspiration to carry us forward.

Let us not forget that if we did not have the drive to succeed, we would not get very far. Make getting motivated a regular part of your routine. Imagine, reimagine, and then put our thought into action. If we keep this in our minds throughout the day, we will find it much simpler to live a more fulfilling life, scale new heights, and develop into a more admirable person overall.

3) Have a Positive Attitude to Begin the Day

Have you ever found that you had slept on the wrong side of the bed and woke up? The most of us have, at one point or another, and it has lasted for the entirety of the day. If being negative may follow us from the time we wake up to the moment we go to sleep at night, then being positive can do the same. To get our day off to a good start, let's all put on a cheery face and think positively. A shift to the appropriate mentality at the appropriate moment can be a game-changer.

4) Picture it. Our Accomplishment One of the most effective ways for us to motivate ourselves to work is to imagine how good it would feel when we have successfully completed all of the tasks that have been assigned to us. When we have finished what we set out to do, it is a wonderfully satisfying feeling because all of the weight and tension that has been on our minds simply evaporates into thin air.

Thinking about how it felt to complete our task would undoubtedly make us feel better about ourselves. Knowing that some enlightenment is waiting for you at the finish line will make you feel empowered, determined, and motivated to complete the task, regardless of how tedious or difficult the task may be.

5. Keeping Oneself Motivated While Working

It has been said that more work is completed on the day before we are supposed to go on annual leave than on any other day. Since this is the case, why not make the entire day productive and feel great as a result of your efforts?

There are certain days when working at the office may be such a chore that by the time you walk out the door of the building, you may already feel as though you've used up every last bit of energy that you have. This is a common occurrence that may happen to anyone, particularly when there are a lot of deadlines to meet, our boss is breathing down our necks, and there is a ton of paperwork. In any case, we must not allow ourselves to become disheartened by the situation.

This is quite normal, therefore there is no need to be concerned about it. Since work is what it is, this kind of thing generally occurs pretty much every day. The way in which we perceive things, on the other hand, is what sets us apart. When we look at it more closely, we discover that the workers at the bottom of the pecking order typically view their jobs as little more than work.

On the other hand, the chief executive officer (CEO) and other higher-ups are somewhat visionaries in the sense that they see a different side of things, which is one of the reasons why they are the leaders of a company. By pushing ourselves to do better at work, we can work our way up the food chain and earn more money.

Be discerning. When choosing your companions, exercise extreme caution. You are a perfect reflection of the individuals you spend the most time with. Get rid of the negative influences that people have had on you throughout your life. Your attire, if you will. When you buy a brand, you give off an impression of who you are. Be conscious of the people your money is going to and the causes it is supporting when making financial decisions. Your selection of groceries leaves a trace, just like every other transaction you make. Purchase food that has been grown in a sustainable manner and is beneficial to your body. Be conscious of the fact that taking in new sights and noises can invigorate your spirit and move your ingenuity. Take note of the programs and channels that you tune in to and watch.

Focus inward. One more time, people all over the world are eager to share their wisdom with you, and there are numerous paths that have been paved for you to follow on your journey through life. If you live your life intentionally and choose your own path, pay attention to what other people tell you to do, but ultimately, you need to look within yourself to find the answers that are right for you. Get in touch with your inner voice by going inward. Have faith in the voice that lives inside you.

The welfare of society depends on you maintaining a firm grasp on whatever it is you currently possess. In any event, there are a great many things that are deserving of being given up. It is well worth it to let go of your pessimism and judgment toward other people and the circumstances they find themselves in. You will not find success with either option. In addition, it is beneficial to cut off any connections. Let go of the requirement that you must remain attached to your wishes, aims, dreams, and goals. Keep working toward the goals you have set for yourself in your day-to-day life, but don't be afraid to let go along the way. You don't need to have a firm grasp on something in order to tie your sense of self-worth to your level of achievement in a given endeavor.

Respect the present moment. You are most likely residing in a moment that has already occurred or that has not yet been conceived about. Will it locate you at this time? In the words of Eckhart Tolle, "Anything the present time has, embrace it as if you had opted for it." Avoid making the same errors and having the same negative experiences as before, as well as thinking about the agony over and over in your head. There is no need to be concerned about things that have not yet occurred. Focus on the here and now. Keep your attention on the task at hand.

Demonstrations of absolution performed repeatedly and routinely. We continue to harbor thoughts of bitterness and engage in harmful activities, firmly grasping the coal of equity in the palms of our hands. When we stubbornly cling to our hostility and refuse to make amends for wrongs committed against us, the burning coal eventually consumes our very own hands. Individuals should be forgiven and cleared of blame for the many small offenses they have committed against you.

Focus on the things that you already own. If we focused more on the successes and experiences we've already had in life, rather than the ones we're still striving for, don't you think it would be more enjoyable? The more we focus on what we already possess and express gratitude for it, the less we will operate from a place of lack or want in our daily lives. When we concentrate on what we already own, we feel more content.

Be generous with your gifts. Giving is the only situation in which it is appropriate to share without expecting anything in return. If you are in a position to serve, you should. There is not a strong reason to consider assisting other people who are in a difficult situation. When you are helping someone else into a building, it is almost impossible to make a mistake. Every day, make it a point to look for additional ways you may assist others.

Exercise some compassion. Develop some compassion not only for other people but also for yourself. Put an end to your perfectionist tendencies and stop setting such stringent expectations for yourself. Love should come from within, and one should cultivate joy in order to purge oneself of pessimism. Extend your capacity for empathy to include other people. Instead of feeling contempt and passing judgment, strive to empathize with them and try to understand the circumstances in which they find themselves.

Take in the serene atmosphere. The globe can be compared to a noisy bazaar. Your brain is as well. The most effective method to restrict both your thinking and your life is to increase your rate of contemplation. Find ways to stay still and make it a practice so that you can become more conscious of your own reflections. Being careful enables one to live their life in a more considered manner. Clarity and voluntary action are both prompted by practicing mindfulness. You should not worry when the television is turned off and there is no loud music playing.

Maintain an awareness of your ego. Our deeper selves like to take control of our lives and steer the course of events, but only if and until we are able to expose them for who and what they really are. By remembering it, you stop the personality from taking over and becoming dominant. Your ego needs to be able to take control of a room, dominate a conversation, feel dominating, and possess your personality. Be conscious of the fact that the ego is the source of your feelings of superiority, judgment, and hostility. Always be on the lookout for evidence of the inner self, and use this information to your advantage when you try to win the affection of the elusive creature.

Take responsibility for what you say. Be deliberate and insufficient with your use of language. Be aware that words have the power to hurt. If there is an alternative way to phrase it that will be easier on someone's ears and heart, then you should try to phrase it in a more pleasant way. If there is a way to converse that causes less damage and more movement, then you should choose that strategy. Consider opting for silence instead of words if the situation calls for something more subdued. Words have meanings, and those meanings have consequences. Be familiar with the language that you employ.

Replace anger with admiration to calm the situation. Be glad to observe the fury when it reaches the point where it explodes like a volcano spewing lava. Observe it while it repeatedly cleans to obtain a better understanding of the source of your aggravation. Make plans to sit with your anger for a while so that you can figure out how to deal with it more effectively. When you don't receive what you want, anger quickly follows. Or, on the other hand, when somebody is unable to fulfill your expectations or causes you to feel disappointment. Awakening to the reality that nobody can make you angry is a necessary step. Nobody except you can understand the things that set you off and make you frustrated. Do you feel as though in order to continue living a conscious existence, you have to transform into a profound and illuminated being? No.

You can make an effort every day to deal with the challenge of continuing to live a conscious life. Having the intention to live a life with deeper meaning is the first step toward practicing conscious living. When you give more thought to how you conduct your life, you give yourself the gift of more pleasure and contentment.

The Language Of The Body And Its Physiology

As I sat there, I had an awful feeling on the inside. This manager had a frowning expression on her face.

I hadn't been able to provide her with enough of an update, and she had exceptionally high expectations.

As her behavior became increasingly hostile, I found that I was experiencing rising levels of anxiety and tension. When I explained what I planned to do, I made an effort to be as cool and collected as possible while I spoke. This bolstered her belief in my capabilities, and she expressed happiness as she exited the meeting.

There was another time, not involving the same person as the one described above, in which there was an incident at work. The second example is a date, and it goes like this...

She started probing me a little bit in order to gain a better understanding of who I am.

She was obviously putting me to the test by asking me some questions that were fairly difficult. I simply stood there, smiling and maintaining eye contact with the person behind me. On the inside, however, I wasn't feeling this way at all.

At the end of the date, she told me that she had a romantic interest in me, and after that, we went on another date together.

What do these things indicate?

Well, what they illustrate is that even though circumstances may be difficult, maintaining composure and being cool under pressure is a lot better and can bring about positive outcomes. Therefore, sometimes it is necessary to fake confidence in order to get more durable outcomes. When we are successful with other individuals, our level of confidence around those individuals rises, which in turn helps our sense of self-worth.

Negative feelings can be expressed, but only at the appropriate moment and in the appropriate setting. This can be challenging at times. These could include writing them down in a journal, discussing them with a trusted friend, or simply spending time alone with oneself.

I've been in situations when people lost their cool with other people and let their vulnerabilities show. I've also been in those situations. Insecurities are something that we all struggle with, although some are more severe than others.

It is best practice to recognize them and address them instead of ignoring them; nonetheless, there is a time and a place for everything. Both sides will benefit nothing from individuals falling out with one another or from an outburst of emotion.

Work instead on visualizing prospective challenging circumstances whenever it is possible to do so. This is something that I do every morning. Then you should focus on improving your body language. How would someone who exudes confidence handle this situation, and how would they behave? When I think about this, the body language of Harvey Specter comes to mind.

Another aspect of this is that if we alter our physiology, we may also alter our state of mind. Although it goes without saying, if you are having trouble dealing with problems in your thoughts over the long term, you will need to practice some of the additional exercises that are included in this book. Receiving good physiology on a frequent basis can be helpful as one.

When I'm in a bad mood, one of the exercises I do is jump up and down while smiling; this transforms the negative energy I'm experiencing into the good energy I need to get through the day.

This is helpful for getting back up after feeling down, but if you want your happy sentiments to be more lasting, you will need to engage in positive physiological activities on a daily basis.

In addition to this, I find that going for a brisk walk first thing in the morning to be beneficial. I also make it a habit to dance for five minutes first thing in the morning, regardless of how I am feeling;

by the time I have finished, I am significantly happier.

Consider some difficult circumstances as your assignment for this step. Begin making a list of the ways in which you would behave if you could be completely honest with yourself. Pay special attention to the way you carry yourself physically.

Second, I want you to dedicate each day to concentrating on a different facet of body language, whether it be maintaining eye contact, walking erect, power posing, or sitting upright. Choose one, keep practicing it until it becomes second nature, and then move on to the next.

Reorganization Of Thought Processes

Restructuring one's cognitive processes is a frequent practice that is implemented in a variety of therapeutic modalities, most notably those that are founded on the principles of cognitive therapy. It is quite effective, and you will need to learn to acknowledge the strength that it brings to the battleground in order to be successful. One of the most powerful tools you have at your disposal for improving yourself is the ability to reorganize your thoughts, or more accurately, the capacity to literally shape them. The only thing you need to do is educate yourself on how to start exercising control over the thoughts that you have.

The power of positivity

You predicted well; positivity will, of its own accord, counteract the negativity that is present in your thoughts. It is something that can be used on a regular basis to determine what it is that you need to know about how you can think and how you can handle situations that are more challenging. You will discover how to change your attitude quickly and easily once you learn the appropriate way to think positively, which will teach you how to alter your mindset. The only thing you need to do is replace that negativity with positivity, and everything else will fall into place on its own.

Being mindful

The practice of stopping what you're doing and paying attention in the here and now is called mindfulness. When you take a moment to pause what you're doing and truly pay attention to what's going on in the world around you, it's typically easy to pinpoint exactly how you're sensation. When you are aware of how you are feeling, you are in a better position to determine what is leading to the mental processes that you are experiencing, and you are also in a better position to figure out how to respond appropriately to the person with whom you are now dealing. Consider the following: if you were furious, you would be able to calmly remind yourself that you are, in fact, angry and then utilize the information that you have to prevent yourself from lashing out angrily by telling yourself that you are angry.

thankfulness If you're looking for one more popular strategy that will help you maintain a positive frame of mind, you can count on practicing thankfulness. When you are able to pause and acknowledge what it is that you already possess, you will be in a position to remind yourself to hold on to that possession. You can try to keep in mind that things could be worse, but they could also be better in certain respects. It's possible that you have a wonderful friend or that you count yourself really fortunate to be in the relationship that you are currently in. Both of these things could be the case. Even if you are in the middle of a disagreement right now, you may reassure yourself that the situation is not hopeless and that you still have access to that which is positive. The negative feelings that come from not being able to acquire what you want and from the perception that you are not living up to expectations can be greatly alleviated by practicing gratitude. while you are in a state of thankfulness, you are aware that there is still something to look forward to, and while this is the case, you will naturally gravitate toward a more positive outlook. This method, like the others that we have discussed thus far, can be applied constructively in ways that will be to your advantage as well as the advantage of individuals in your immediate environment.

The Influence of Feelings on Both Health and Illness

The expression of one's feelings is an important component of one's day-to-day life. They are obligatory in our life due to the fact that they typically have a driving influence on a person and because they are unavoidable occurrences. However, the importance of emotions is often limited to some particular degree, and when that degree is exceeded, the feeling can be seen as detrimental. This is due to the fact that an intense sensation can lead to the modification of an individual's normally functioning, which in turn can be deemed harmful.

Keeping an emotion going for an extended period of time can also mess with the way organs in the body work. Because of the excessive physiological changes that come about as a result of protracted emotions, they are unable to perform their duties in a broad sense. Extreme emotional upheavals are what lead to the development of psychosomatic diseases. Emotional stress is linked to a variety of illnesses, including colitis, peptic ulcers, migraines, headaches, low or high blood pressure, skin problems, and even high or low blood sugar. Continuous exposure to a certain emotion can also make it difficult to treat the underlying disease that's causing the problem.

A Detailed Breakdown of How to Keep Your Cool Under Pressure

It is impossible to avoid becoming emotional, yet it is possible to exercise control over how we respond to significant feelings. Because people's moods influence how they see others around them and how they interact with those they come into contact with, it is a crucial talent to be able to function well even when feeling a range of different feelings. As a result, individuals shouldn't strive to stifle or ignore their feelings, but rather they should focus on learning how to better manage how they react to the feelings that they experience. It is important not to avoid dealing with one's feelings since, if one does so, dysfunctional coping mechanisms may eventually be developed in response to the unresolved emotional issues.

The ability to skillfully manage one's emotions can be achieved by following these steps.

Put a name to your feelings: To be able to alter how a person is feeling, one must first be able to accurately assess what it is that they are going through at any given moment. This can aid in comprehending the feeling that reveals itself whenever one is experiencing a particular way. It is also necessary for an individual, in order for them to comprehend emotion, to pay careful attention to whatever is taking place within themselves. When a feeling is given a name, a person is better able to recognize the impact that a certain sensation has on the choices they make in their day-to-day lives.

Reframing the thought: Emotions always play a role in how a person interprets certain events in their life. For instance, if a student is feeling worried and they receive a notice that their lecturer will be calling them, they can infer that they have done poorly on an exam or that they will be disciplined for their behavior. On the other hand, when they are in a good mood and receive a message that is similar to the one they received before, they can believe that they are being rewarded for having successfully completed a test. To have a more optimistic perspective on the world, it is necessary to learn how to control one's feelings. Reframing one's thinking can assist in the development of a realistic picture, which can lead to an increase in one's ability to manage the emotional experiences that they are exposed to. This is something that may be accomplished by looking at things from a variety of angles and coming up with new points of view.

Participating in mental exercise: When someone is going through a negative emotion, they may withdraw from others and focus their attention inside, or they may even complain a great deal to other people. However, this kind of behavior keeps a person mired in a negative mindset, and the ideal course of action—the only one that really matters—is to engage in constructive activities. One should consider the activities that bring them joy and make an effort to participate in those pursuits. For instance, one can go for a stroll, meditate on a few positive things, call a friend and talk about pleasant scenarios, or simply listen to some uplifting music. All of these things have the potential to improve one's mood.

Keep your feelings and your actions separate: Emotions are quite potent, and maintaining control over them may be quite a difficult task. In this scenario, it is absolutely necessary to have an understanding of the indicators that guide you to act in a specific manner. Having the ability to control your emotions requires that you be able to differentiate between what you are experiencing and how you are acting. It is important to refrain from doing anything physically taxing whenever one is experiencing a strong emotion.

Consistency in the practice of emotional regulation skills One of the most helpful things in terms of gaining control over one's feelings is maintaining a consistent practice of emotional regulation skills anytime that feeling presents itself. Maintaining control of one's emotions over time enables one to develop mental resilience, which in turn fosters an increased sense of self-assurance when dealing with a variety of feelings. By acting in this manner, one can improve their chances of making decisions and selections that are not influenced by their feelings.

Recognizing The Degree Of Self-Confidence You Possess

It's possible that you're curious about the origins of your current level of self-confidence. This is influenced by a great number of different things. When we are approximately two or three years old, we typically start to establish our sense of self-confidence. This is true even though it isn't fair to blame our parents for every single issue that we struggle with in the present day. Consequently, our parents have a significant impact on the amount of self-confidence that we possess at this point in our lives. Children who are regularly reaffirmed of their value and worth are more likely to have healthy levels of self-esteem as adults.

Children are more likely to have issues with their self-confidence if their parents have a tendency to be excessively critical and are quick to point out deficiencies or perceived failings in their children. Right now is not the time to be upset with or blame your parents for the situation you find yourself in. On the other hand, if you do have children, the information in this passage ought to serve as a wake-up call for you.

As you get older, the people in your social circle might also have an effect on your level of self-confidence. You should be aware that in some situations, peers have a more significant impact on a person's life than their parents do before you rush to pass judgment on your own parents. There is a good reason why wise persons will tell you to be selective in the people you keep as friends. Kids have a pattern of occasionally behaving in a cruel manner. Your self-confidence would never have a chance to flourish if, first, you did not have parents who bolstered your self-esteem at home and then, second, you found yourself in a peer group that was equally lacking in support.

Adults have a better ability to recognize unhealthy relationships, but it is not always simple to decide what to do about them, particularly if they have caused damage to their sense of self-confidence. You need to have the self-assurance to inform a friend that spending time with him isn't good for either of you. If he is unable to give you support or encouragement, there is no need for him to be a part of your inner circle. The truth is that as you start down the path of boosting your self-confidence, you may find that you have to perform a little housecleaning in terms of your circle of friends. You don't need to be concerned about being lonely because, further on in the book, we are going to talk about how to meet new people who will accept you for who you are.

When you have eliminated the negative influences in your life, it will be time to take the actions necessary to liberate yourself from all of the unhelpful and undesired negative feelings you have been harboring. Continue reading this article if you are prepared to begin the process of improving your self-esteem right away.

It is vital for us to possess specified quantities of self-discipline, talents, capability, determination, and most importantly, self-confidence, in order for us to be able to attain a particular objective in our lives. This particular form of assurance originates from the individual's possession of the appropriate forms of skills, in addition to having a distinct understanding of the objectives that need to be accomplished. A skilled mind and body cannot supply an individual with what it needs to perform to the best of their ability until these are backed up by self-confidence. Only then will an individual be able to function to the greatest of their abilities. If we are completely honest with ourselves, our sense of self-worth serves as the fulcrum upon which the entire creative and analytical capacity of the human brain turns. A lack of self-confidence has the capacity to substantially impair the workings of not only the mind, but also the body, which in turn leads to some devastating failures. This is for the reason that a lack of self-confidence has the potential to impair greatly the workings of not just the mind, but also the body.

If we lack the necessary amount of self-assurance, we will never be able to realize our full potential in this life and accomplish the wonderful things we envision for ourselves. Even if you have the most impressive set of skills and attributes in the world, if you lack self-confidence, you won't be able to succeed. This is due to the fact that having poor self-esteem can make it impossible for you to progress in life, which in turn makes it impossible for you to take any initiative at all. When it comes time to make individual choices, it's almost as if your mind and body go into a state of paralysis as a result of it. You need to keep in mind that this life works marvelously for those who are confident, since confidence has the capacity to create or shatter your experience in a way that nothing else can. You need to keep this in mind at all times. If you want to bring out the fighter that's been dormant inside of you, you need to have confidence in yourself.

You need to keep in mind the fundamental truth that our level of self-confidence, or self-esteem, as some people may refer to it, has the capacity to impact each and every facet of our lives. This is something that you must keep in mind at all times. To what extent we are able to accomplish in our life is directly related to this particular component. The key to understand about having self-confidence is that it has an effect on you not just psychologically and emotionally, but also, in certain cases, physically. People are able to have optimistic and even realistic perspectives of not only their life, but also of every scenario that they come into contact with because they have adopted an attitude that makes it feasible for them to do so. Self-confidence, on the other hand, does not in any way imply that a person is capable of accomplishing everything in their life; rather, it merely gives a person the ability to put forth their best effort in everything that they do without having to question their ability or even give it a second thought at all. Having self-confidence simply gives a person the potential to put forth their best effort in everything that they do.

People who struggle with low levels of self-confidence tend to be overly reliant on the acceptance of others throughout their lives. This includes approval of what they should do, how they should act, and even what they should wear. This is a terrible reality that plagues many who suffer from low levels of self-confidence. They have no control over their lives in any way, shape, or form, and they typically do not believe it is possible for them to ever achieve any kind of success in life. Even if they are given a compliment, there is a good chance that they will disregard it or even make light of it for the simple reason that they consider themselves unworthy of receiving it. Instead, they have a propensity to respond to the compliment with some kind of self-deprecating statement, which, as a result of the harsh reaction, makes others less likely to provide kind words in the future due to the severity of the reaction. People who are self-assured, on the other hand, disregard what other people have to say because they have unwavering faith in their own capabilities. These people are comfortable with who they are, and they don't believe it's necessary for them to change who they are in order to fit in with the preferences of others in order to be accepted in society.

In point of fact, the feeling of certainty that one possesses regarding who they are and the capacity to love and accept oneself, flaws and all, are the cornerstones of confidence. Because you have lived your life in an honest manner, maintaining your integrity, and centering your decisions on the principles that are important to you, you are able to look at yourself with a sense of self-respect and an optimistic realism. A self-assured person is aware of who they are and the kind of life they want to lead, and they are able to quickly recover from setbacks and errors in judgment with an adequate amount of mourning and introspection.

Goalsetting

One must have drive in order to have happiness and contentment in life. We are fundamentally fueled by motivation, which gives us the desire to look forward and dream higher. We are compelled to move forward by the power. Whatever the case may be, why do we need to adapt to the new circumstances? Different things motivate different people to progress. Some people alter their behavior because they would rather avoid confronting the suffering in their lives. Some people make a change because they are sick and tired of being disappointed. For instance, receiving grades that are less than exceptional can help us realize the necessity of working hard while we are being tested, which in turn can motivate us to make changes. In addition, obligations can motivate us to seek out new career opportunities or to pursue more than one occupation at a time.

The world is filled to the brim with cynicism, and regardless of what other people may say, we need to confront this hostility and work toward overcoming it. Whatever the case may be, the decision ultimately rests with you. Who is more accountable for your life—you or the environment in which you live? As soon as you come to the realization that you are responsible for whatever occurs, you will put your foot down and overcome the hostility that surrounds you.

It is easy for us to stay within the comfort zone of our typical circle of acquaintances. On the other hand, have you ever tried breaking out of your typical circle of acquaintances to get a glimpse of what is beyond? What specifically prevents you from acting in this manner? Are you frustrated? Any concerns? What a disgrace! The first and most important thing that you need to do in order to grow yourself is to have a goal and to make a few goals for yourself. As soon as you are aware of your destination, you will be able to properly maintain your concentration and will not allow yourself to get sidetracked by anything that gets in your way.

The next step is to establish some concrete plans that will enable you to make progress toward your goals. When you are arranging things, avoid just thinking inside the comfortable boundaries of your typical sphere of experience. Step outside of the box in order to discover a more modern version of yourself. Determine the differences between your problems and your limitations, then devise solutions to overcome them. Make sure that you are aware of your faults and that you are working to improve them while maintaining the moral characteristics that are important to you.

Carry out the plan you've established, and don't worry about whether or not it will be successful. You are not going to be broken by disappointments; on the contrary, they will strengthen you. You should rework your arrangements in the event that they do not meet your needs, identify any escape clauses, and implement tactics that will aid you in overcoming these conditions. Each failure teaches you a valuable lesson about what you should avoid, and moreover, it provides you with a significant workout. Get as much benefit as you can from these workouts so that you can re-inforce the more modern version of yourself.

Make an effort to avoid gloomy individuals and factors as much as possible. These kinds of musings and words force you to maintain one eye on the breaking point of your potential and cause you to become more fragile. If you have faith in your plans, you will focus on your course of action and will only make adjustments if you truly feel the need to do so, regardless of what other people may think or say. With this strategy, you will be able to leap over the obstacles that are directly in your path.

In the end, it's important to learn to appreciate life and accept incredible things. Your brain will operate more quickly, and success will come your way when you are happy and have something to look forward to. Therefore, cling tenaciously to your ideals, accept responsibility for your life, and move on with the intention of appreciating the journey as the more evolved version of yourself.

How To Improve Your Self-Esteem And Stand Out Despite Being An Introvert

Even if many people are perplexed by introverts and their behavior, they are still a special and distinct personality type. The majority of parties will have them standing around the outside of the venue. People will have the incorrect impression that they are timid, despite the fact that this is not the case. Simply said, introverts have a finite amount of social energy that they can waste before they feel the need to retreat and regain their strength.

Because the majority of people in the world are extroverts, it may be more challenging for introverts to establish new acquaintances or advance their careers in an environment dominated by extroverts. However, it is best for them to remain in their introverted lane because attempting to portray themselves as anything other than what they are would be too difficult and would imply that they are not being true to who they are.

It is necessary for many introverts to have their self-esteem bolstered in order for them to be able to shine as who they truly are. This is not an impossible task, despite the fact that it may be a challenging procedure.

Being an introvert is not a reflection of one's morality; rather, it is a characteristic of one's personality, just like being an extrovert. While Eastern countries have traditionally been more accommodating of introverts, Western societies are known for being more outgoing and enthusiastic.

Countries like China, Korea, and Thailand are safe havens for introverts because they do not make introverts feel inferior; instead, introverts are seen as perfect personalities in these countries. The people who live in these kinds of countries have the belief that being restrained and thoughtful is a virtue that exemplifies a decent person's character.

Introverts can shine in a variety of different contexts and settings.

Maintain a constructive outlook on your individuality - You should not feel bad about being an introvert. It's not a defect; it's a feature of your personality. People who are more reserved are not alone. In point of fact, there are more of you than you think there are.

It is important to refrain from being overly judgmental of yourself and to acknowledge the possibility that you may struggle with performing some tasks. It's possible that conversing with complete strangers is not your strong point, and that giving a speech in front of an audience is more terrifying to you than going through a haunted house. Recognize whatever it is that holds you back, but avoid being too hard on yourself in the process.

Recognize the introverted side of your personality – There are many distinct types of people who are considered to be introverts. One of the most fundamental characteristics of introversion is the need to recharge one's batteries by either spending time alone or with a close friend who provides emotional support.

The practice of taking in information before providing a response is also an essential component. You feel the need to give some thought to what is being conveyed to you. For instance, an extrovert would read an article online and then immediately reply with their thoughts and feelings regarding the subject matter of the piece. You, on the other hand, want to go away and give yourself some time to reflect on what was discussed in the article before you offer your viewpoint. That is, assuming you even choose to voice an opinion on the matter. Because you are sensitive about protecting your private, it's possible that you won't be able to talk about what's on your mind. (2017) (Boyes, 2013)

Every introvert is unique in their own way. You are therefore free to cherry-pick the recommendations that are applicable to you and disregard the rest of the content as irrelevant.

Try not to judge yourself by the standards of extroverted people. There's a good chance that, despite being an introvert, you've fantasized about being the life of the party and the center of everyone's attention in a dream. You are the one who everyone listens to as you recount your most recent exploits regarding your trip to Australia, including where you went, what you did, and who you met.

You should be aware that despite the fact that it may appear to be beneficial to be the life of the party wherever you go, being an introvert also offers its own set of benefits that should not be overlooked.

Take, for instance, the scenario in which you have recently released a book that has been very successful and has become a smash all over the country.

Your publisher then notifies you that you will be embarking on a book tour. Do you think you'll appreciate being the center of attention and doing countless interviews?

If you're more of an introvert than extrovert, you probably don't want to be put in the situation described in the previous sentence. If you are a true introvert, you would much rather get the recognition you deserve from a safe distance than up close and personal.

Recognize that you are the type of person who is able to read between the lines more attentively than those who are given more of the spotlight, and be okay with that. (Hayward, 2018) (Hayward)

The Distinction Between Having Low Self-Confidence And Naturally Being An Introvert

People who are confident in themselves and their abilities are certain not just that what they do and how they do it is correct, but also that most people will like them. If either of these components is absent from your toolkit of self-assurance, it's time to get to work on filling the gap.

Start a blog. Introverts appreciate the opportunity to spend time by themselves to reflect and record their ideas. The world of online blogging that exists now is ideal for introverts who want to express themselves.

Even while extroverts are more often praised for their outgoing personalities, introverts can still make an influence through the use of social media.

Having a demeanor that is more restrained can be beneficial to establishing credibility. People that yell the loudest are more likely to get noticed in our environment, whereas introverts take the time to be aware and put in the effort to genuinely listen to what others have to say. As a result, these insights can be adapted into pieces of literature that have the potential to profoundly affect the reader.

Introverts tend to spend a lot of time thinking about things they've seen or heard, so they need to be encouraged to use their creative side. As was stated before, this type of creativity is beneficial when it comes to writing a blog, and it also has the potential to uncover other aspects of a person's personality.

Most introverts have a greater capacity for original thought. Studies have shown that introverts are able to put more thought into the work that they do on their creative projects than other people can.

1.3 The Art of Leadership

Leadership requires having faith in oneself as a person who is able to guide people in the right direction. It is important to remember that you should always follow your gut feelings, regardless of the circumstances you find yourself in. This won't be the case in every situation. In life, we will frequently be required to act as followers or to submit to the decisions of others. When it is your turn to be a leader, you must, on the other hand, allow yourself to be the leader that you truly are on the inside.

Because of the unique viewpoints that each of us possesses, there is the possibility for anyone to take on a leadership role. Every one of us has our own unique perspective, set of routines, and strategies for bringing about change, as well as our own unique interpretation of the word. This indicates that each of us has a feeling of self to the extent that we are able to achieve it, and this can enable you to provide yourself the opportunity to share others into your personal vision and direct individuals to assist the group in achieving anything.

When you are just being yourself, you leave yourself open to attack. Because the rest of the world will see you for who you really are when you expose your innermost thoughts and deeds to them, you can feel more confident in who you are as a person. Let's take a moment to consider your personal outlook on how you should relate to the "world." Some people have a perspective on the world that can be summarized as follows: "The world is a place that can provide a lot of opportunities, along with other dangers, that outweigh the negative aspects of the world." The perceptions of other people are not nearly as upbeat as our own. Some people have the mentality that the world is always conspiring against them. They are under the impression that everyone else in the world is out to get them and put them in their place. They are unaware of how little they are in the grand scheme of things. Understanding how insignificant you are in the grand scheme of things can assist one in gaining perspective.

When you have a clear picture of who you are and where you fit in the world, you can finally start to feel confident about yourself. When you have a sense of perspective, you are aware of the areas in which you excel as well as those in which you struggle. We are not going to be discussing narcissism in this conversation. Narcissism causes a person to become preoccupied with themselves and to believe that they are superior to everyone else in the world. That is not something that will be discussed in this setting. We are discussing a confident demeanor that is both warm and assertive, giving others the impression that they can trust you and follow your lead in whatever endeavor you propose.

And this is what leadership is: having influence over other individuals. It means distinguishing yourself from the rest of the throng, making sure that you are seen and heard, and inspiring other people to follow your vision. If you do not believe in what you are selling, then you are nothing more than a simple con artist. Kindness requires genuineness, as does the awareness of what it is you hope to achieve from a certain circumstance.

When you are self-assured, mindful, and true to who you are, you will be compelled to believe in whatever it is that you honestly and deeply believe, and you will have the ability to persuade others to do the same. Although there are those who are able to persuade others of things in which they do not have faith, this is not the most effective strategy for swaying other people's opinions. Individualism, tranquility, and thoughtfulness are qualities that ought to permeate this endeavor at all times.

In all honesty, you need to think about the long game when it comes to influence. Keep in mind that it is far simpler to persuade a friend than a stranger when you are trying to sway someone's opinion. Therefore, make an effort to include them to your circle of friends. You have to work on developing your social skills to the point where you can achieve this, which is to win someone's favor and have them like you. Alternately, you should probably think of it as giving people the opportunity to like you. To be able to pull this off, you need to have a high level of self-assurance and the realization that if you behave in a way that is true to who you are, the vast majority of people in the world will find you to be likeable.

Once you have established a friendship with another person, you will naturally begin to trust one another. You have faith that they will not take advantage of you in any way and you feel safe with them. When you have let down your defenses to such an extent that people can see that you do not intend to hurt them, this is when you have the most potential to influence other people. People will not trust you, and they will be unable to be swayed by you, if they believe that you want to inflict pain on them or exploit them for the purpose of gaining financial gain or other resources. If you develop positive relationships with other people, you will have the ability to persuade others to act in a way that is hopeful and positive.

We can't stress this point enough: if you want to influence people, you have to be yourself. This is not as straightforward as it may first appear. For instance, when an actor is playing a role and doing a really good job of it, even though they are acting as if they are another person, they are still being themselves, which is why they are so amazing at what they do. They are putting their hearts and souls into it and bringing it to life by being truthful and remaining true to who they are. This is just one illustration among many. It's possible that you do things that seem completely out of character, but in reality they're exactly what you need to do in order to be true to who you are.

Fear

In this chapter, we are going to discuss fear and the many different ways in which it can prevent you from moving forward in life. Fear is something that happens to all of us; it is something that is intrinsically a part of us. It dates back to the days of early humans and beyond, when we required our bodies to tell us that there was something that we should avoid telling us when there was a threat, and it exists to let us know when there is a threat. It was a matter of life and death at that point in history; thus, it was very necessary for our bodies to send the message that we should flee by making us feel afraid. You have probably become familiar with the expression "fight or flight" in the past. This is the precise concept that is being referred to by that word. You will experience terror whenever your body is alerted to a potential threat or danger. Your body will then have to determine whether it will fight or run away, and it will perform one of these things after making its decision.

This is not necessarily the case in modern times. When we experience dread in the modern world, it is not usually because of something that could end our lives. The fear that we experience ultimately prevents us from participating in things such as new experiences or putting ourselves in circumstances that are unfamiliar to us. Even though these scenarios probably don't pose any danger to us, when we're scared, we might choose to run, and if we do, we might get hurt.

How Your Fear Is Keeping You From Moving Forward

If you give fear the power to run your life, it may wind up being something that holds you back. In this part of the article, we will discuss how, despite its function as a protective mechanism, fear can make it more difficult for a person to live a life that is pleasant and meaningful.

The Zone of Comfort

We are going to discuss the comfort zone in the next part of this article. Your "comfort zone" is a term that is used to describe the locations, activities, things, people, and everything else in your life with which you have a high level of familiarity and ease. Some people prefer to remain within their comfort zone by declining opportunities that lie outside of it, while others get a kick out of challenging themselves by continually venturing outside of it and forcing themselves to remain uncertain and uneasy. For instance, if you recently met someone and they invite you to go out to a bar with them and their friends, some of whom you do not know, in a neighborhood that you have never been to before, you should probably decline the invitation. Under these circumstances, participating in this event would unquestionably put anyone outside of their comfort zone. You are now presented with a choice: either you accept the invitation and attend the event, despite the fact that everything about it, including the individuals there, is unfamiliar to you, or you decline the invitation and stay home. The second choice is to politely decline the offer and either hang out with individuals you already know in your immediate area or head back home to unwind in your room. One of these alternatives is driven by fear or by the fear of stepping outside of the comfort zone, while the other option is motivated by curiosity and a want to step outside of the comfort zone. Neither of these choices is necessarily a poor one; nonetheless, one choice is driven by fear and the other is driven by a desire to walk outside of the comfort zone.

If you give in to the fight-or-flight response that your body possesses, even in situations that offer no risk, it can lead you to a life of saying no to every new experience or challenge, and it can keep you trapped in your comfort zone for the rest of your life. While there are circumstances that require you to give in to this response, there are also circumstances that do not. In the aforementioned scenario, if the individual decides to turn down the invitation because the experience will expose them to too many novel aspects, they will have given in to the fight or flight response of their body and will have picked the flight option. On the other hand, if they are aware that the prospect of engaging in these novel activities causes them to feel anxious, they can choose to go ahead and do so nonetheless in order to broaden their horizons, secure in the knowledge that their choice will most likely not result in their death.

As a result, anxiety will end up preventing you from moving on if you choose to decline this invitation because of the other things to which you will inevitably decline. It's possible that you might have met someone at this pub with whom you would have had an incredible connection, but because you turned down the opportunity, you have deprived yourself of the option to do so. It's possible that you would have discovered a band that you really liked if you had gone to this bar to see them perform live, but since you didn't, you have no idea who they are. It's possible that you would have visited this new neighborhood, found that you simply adored it, and then made the decision to relocate there when your lease was up. Because you didn't go, you can't say for sure whether or not you would have enjoyed staying in this neighborhood. All of these possibilities and more exist in any given circumstance, but the fact that this opportunity involves so many exciting new things makes the likelihood of their occurring significantly higher. When you stick to your own neighborhood and socialize with individuals you already know, the likelihood of making unexpected discoveries drops dramatically. You are preventing yourself from experiencing many new things that could significantly enrich your life if you stick to what is familiar to you and stay within the confines of your comfort zone. This is true regardless of whether or not you feel like you are currently living a full life.

Putting Your Objectives Down In Writing

Worksheets for goal setting are useful tools that can guide you through each step of the goal-setting process and assist you in formulating a strategy that will increase the likelihood of your dream becoming a reality. These worksheets can be found online or in books.

1. Creating a goal-setting worksheet will make it easier for you to see the larger picture. They are wonderful tools for visualizing the future and seeing yourself, or who you have the potential to become, in a few years' time in the future. They can help guide your thoughts and life patterns in a certain direction so that you can make decisions that are appropriate in light of your ultimate objective.

2. Completing a goal-setting worksheet will assist you in defining your

objectives as well as determining the reasons "why" these particular objectives are significant. Meaningful objectives are essential to the success of any goal-setting endeavor.

The forms will guide you through a series of precise steps that will require you to reflect on your vision, your priorities, and your end goal in order to complete them. You will have a more in-depth understanding of yourself, and as a result, you will be able to bring greater clarity and focus to the accomplishment of your goals.

3. Creating a goal-setting worksheet will assist you in dividing your overall objective into a series of smaller steps that are more feasible to achieve. Understanding the larger picture is essential because, before you can start your journey, you need to have a clear idea of where you want to end up. On the other hand, the journey from where you are to where you want to be can often feel very daunting.

The form enables you to set both short-term and long-term goals, which, when combined, will assist you in realizing your ambitions one step at a time. You can divide a long-term goal into annual, monthly, weekly, and even daily goals; after all, we are capable of doing anything if we take it one day at a time, isn't that right?

You will be asked by the work sheet to list the steps that are necessary to accomplish your strategy and to prioritize your actions in order to achieve success.

4. The goal-setting worksheets that you use will assist you in developing a plan of action and determining the requirements that are necessary to pursue your goal. To accomplish a goal, especially one that is more ambitious or has a longer time frame, requires careful planning.

By laying out the steps that need to be taken in order for you to realize your goals. You will be aware of everything that has to be done and will be able to approach your objective from a very realistic point of view. You will also be able to identify any potential obstacles with the help of this form. This will allow you to be better prepared to deal with any issues that may arise and prevent any unpleasant surprises.

This is especially important if you have a shared goal that you are working toward with someone else, such as a partner in business or a team. Other examples of shared goals include a partnership and a group project. A goal-setting worksheet will detail everyone's duties and ensure that everyone is on the same page on both the overall objective and the plan of action. This will be accomplished by outlining the tasks on a goal-setting worksheet.

5. Goal-setting worksheets offer accountability and make it possible to track your progress toward achieving

your objectives. It is very helpful to have a way to keep track of your progress because life has a lot of distractions, and it is often easy to lose sight of what you are working for. Because of this, it is very beneficial to have a way to track your progress.

Make it a habit to check your worksheets on a regular basis and cross out any goals that you have already achieved. Recognizing and appreciating your successes helps increase your sense of self-worth and encourage you to keep going despite setbacks or discouragement you may have along the way.

Continuous monitoring will not only help you identify where you went wrong but will also help you adjust or revise your course of action as necessary along the way. Keep in mind that your plan has not yet been etched in stone. It will provide you with direction and a framework within which to operate, but there may be times when circumstances need you to be flexible or make changes that will improve your plan of action. In these cases, you should be prepared to adapt your plan accordingly.

6. Creating a goal-setting worksheet can both improve your chances of achieving your objectives and shorten the amount of time it takes to do so. You will be able to maintain your focus and motivation if you have a well-defined plan, especially if your "short-term goals" are attainable, measurable, and provide you the opportunity to celebrate your successes on a regular basis.

Many people never accomplish what they set out to do because they lack the knowledge necessary to turn their dreams into a reality. The forms provide clarity and focus, allowing you to understand precisely what is required of you on a daily, weekly, or monthly basis. You will have an easier time sticking to the plan and seeing it through to completion if you have a crystal clear understanding of the steps you should do.

7. A work sheet for goal setting should include time periods and due dates. A fantastic recipe for success involves partitioning larger goals into more manageable sections, identifying the steps that need to be followed, and establishing a deadline for their completion.

The most effective method for overcoming procrastinationthe key to turning inspiration into motivation is to set a deadline. You might even find that being accountable to someone who will check to ensure that you have fulfilled your time frame guideline is beneficial to you.

Your goal will provide direction, keep you motivated and focused, and help you increase your self-confidence as you monitor your success along the way if you write it down and commit it to paper.

A Value Structure That Is Consistent

Ask yourself the below question before you even begin to practice being respectable in front of other people.

Do I have a coherent system for determining my worth?

Is it possible that some of the concepts that make up your value system contradict one another? It is important that you do not rush to bounce on the ends that do not exist. Keep an eye on your monetary system during the next week.

This serves as an example. Imagine for a moment that, among other tenets, your value system is built on the foundation of two guiding principles. "Be straightforward" in conjunction with "be pleasant to individuals." Finding someone who may potentially go against these principles is difficult. Do these principles perfectly align with one another?

Imagine a situation in which a friend of yours asks for your opinion on a certain business idea, and you are aware that giving your honest evaluation would be detrimental to the person in question. Will you give me the honest scoop? Or, to put it another way, are you going to behave decently?

Image of the Body

Whenever I went to the playground, I would find all of my buddies playing football. Despite this, I had no interest in participating because, back then, I didn't like for either workout or football. Going home, playing video games on my PlayStation, and eating cookie packages was one of my favorite things to do in my free time. My childhood wasn't exactly the picture of health.

A friend of mine approached me one day during lunchtime and remarked, "Jonny, I have to say that you are a bit fat."

This stung my feelings. This caused me a lot of pain. Because of this, I became very silent and made an effort to avoid having conversations with other people in case they insulted me in some way.

I had lost some weight by the time I entered secondary school, and I had also become more active in sports. On the other hand, I struggled with acne and dry skin. When guys would remark things to me like, "what's happening with your skin?," it would make me feel extremely badly about myself, and it would make me not want to go into school.

Then came Ken into the picture.

Ken was a pleasant young man in his twenties who held down a decent career and maintained a small group of close friendships. However, Ken was a somewhat short individual. Because of this, he believed that women would not find him attractive and that he did not measure up to the standards of a desirable man. Ken had a lot of trouble developing a healthy sense of self-esteem, and the fact that he was called "short" by another person was quite painful for him. They probably never even gave it a thought in the first place.

Now, I'll be the first to say that this part is not necessarily one of the most difficult problems for my self-esteem. Despite the fact that I have been obese and covered in spots in the past, I am currently in a state that is considered to be reasonably excellent. It took me a while to accept the fact that I am a good-looking person, despite the fact that I grew up being told by people of the opposite sex that I am pretty. This is because for many years I still felt the same way I did when I was overweight and struggled with acne. My unpleasant experiences from earlier years were buried deep within my subconscious mind, making it difficult for me to move past them.

In addition to this obstacle, I spent years working toward the goal of acquiring a six-pack. To my great relief, I no longer give a damn as long as I'm feeling fantastic. This ties in with the concept of comparing what we see all around us, but when we aren't content with how we seem in relation to others, it can cause us to have significant difficulties with our self-image and, as a result, our esteem.

I've also known some stunningly gorgeous women who were completely unaware of their own attractiveness. They were evaluating themselves in relation to other people. Because of the prevalence of eating disorders such as anorexia and bulimia, maintaining a positive body image can be challenging. Anyone who is having trouble with those will always have my love and support.

When it comes to our body, there are two aspects to consider: the physical and the mental.

1. The things we have control over, and 2. the things we do not.

In many but not all instances, the things we can change about ourselves include our weight and the quality of our skin. There are certain persons who are unable to lose weight because they have conditions such as skin conditions or other diseases.

Things like our natural looks, our height, and the eyes we were born with are characteristics that cannot be altered.

Things that we can change, and questions that we may ask about what we can do. For instance, in order to stay in decent shape these days, I make it a point to work out often and eat healthily. Regarding the things that we are unable to alter, we are required to accept them; this is something that is easier said than done, as is the case with everything else in life; but, ignoring or repressing the things that we are unable to alter will not be helpful. Instead, it is preferable to cultivate an appreciation for one's unique flaws.

Become The Aware Observer Of Your Own Thoughts.

Our thoughts have a tendency to behave in a manner analogous to that of white noise or background music on a moment-to-moment basis. They move fluidly through our thoughts without attracting any attention to themselves. They also do not stick around for an excessive amount of time; if they are permitted to operate independently, thoughts go quickly through our minds. You're debating what to make for dinner one minute, and the next thing you know, you're laughing out loud at something amusing your partner said the previous morning. However, there are instances when we allow ourselves to grow attracted to a specific concept and start to pursue it. Following that one thought leads to another related thought, and then another, and before you know it, you have wasted an hour of your time thinking along these lines. This pattern of behavior can, on sometimes, be rather pleasurable, such as when you allow yourself to become immersed in an enjoyable daydream. However, if you let yourself become emotionally invested in a negative thought, you run the risk of falling down a rabbit hole of negativity very rapidly. At this point, the initial negative thinking, which was more like a snowball at this point, starts to gain momentum and develop into an avalanche.

After it has begun, there is no way to stop an avalanche from occurring. To avoid an avalanche from occurring in the first place is the only way to halt it once it has started. Even if it's not absolutely impossible to put an end to the downward spiral of negative thoughts, it's a lot simpler to halt that spiral before it even begins. How do you go about doing that?

Become aware of

When you are faced with a circumstance, make an effort to observe how you react to it and learn from that experience. Were you irritated when the driver in front of you cut you off in the road? Did the other motorist provoke your fury, or was there a more systemic issue at play?

When you start to assess your circumstances, you can come to the conclusion that things are not as cut and dried as they initially appear to be.

Carry out a Brain-Dumping exercise.

What steps do you take when you see that the trash cans in your home are getting full? It goes without saying that you emptied the garbage container. You don't want the contents of that mound to pour over, do you?

Spend some time writing down your thoughts in order to conduct a successful brain dump.

Your brain works exactly the same way. It's possible that some of the information you have stored in your head won't be helpful to you at all. It's also possible that you're discouraged about your professional or personal life. It may feel like a hurricane is raging in your head at times, and you may find that you are unable to concentrate on a single thought or come up with new ideas during these times. It's possible that just thinking about it will become too much for you.

But why precisely does your brain feel like it can't handle everything?

Imagine if the tabs on your internet browser represent the different thoughts that you have. You have selected a few tabs because you believe they are significant in some way. When new responsibilities enter your life, you find yourself opening even more tabs on your browser. Nevertheless, you fail to remember to close the previous ones. In the end, you find that you have a hundred tabs open, and you are constantly jumping from one tab to the next in an effort to gain some perspective on your thoughts.

The process of getting your thoughts out of your head and onto paper in order to deal with them is referred to as "brain dumping." The procedure enables you to concentrate on one thought at a time and even ranks them in order of importance. So how exactly does one perform a brain dump?

Altering Feelings Through Changes In Behavior

When you take into consideration the James-Lange hypothesis, you are left with the sort of equation that looks like this and it equals emotions:

Stimulus plus the body's response plus the mind's interpretation equals emotion.

You can use this to your advantage by manipulating it. You could use this to break some form of negative emotional habits, such as becoming upset and yelling, which simply makes you get even angrier, or you could use it to stop a phobia through exposure, reminders that you are safe and okay, deep breaths, and plenty of patience on your part. The possibilities are practically endless; you can modify your feelings by changing the things you do. The only thing you need to do to modify the way you feel about a certain stimulus is to adjust both your bodily reaction and how you perceive that reaction as it relates to the stimulus.

Take, for instance, the experience of going through a divorce as an illustration. The mere appearance of your ex-spouse when exchanging custody of your children is enough to make your blood boil, and regardless of what you do or the circumstances under which you see your ex-spouse, you are unable to prevent yourself from being immediately outraged. Perhaps he cheated on you or did something else that left such a huge effect on you that you experience the emotion immediately and to an overwhelming degree at the mere sight of him. This may be the case.

You should get ready for the next time you are going to visit your ex-spouse so that you don't feel unprepared. You are going to take a deep breath the moment you see him. You will posture yourself to be tall and upright. Your shoulders will become more relaxed. You are going to engage in calm eye contact with him. You will not speak louder than necessary. You won't get all worked up over it. You will maintain a steady, calm, and deep breath throughout the exercise, counting to four between each breath if necessary. Make sure you have a plan in place for the next time you have to switch custody of someone. Make a list of the things you need to do. After all, you are aware that it is unhealthy for your children to observe you harboring hatred toward their father, and you do not want to subject them to that experience.

Therefore, when you go back to that location, you should make it a point to try all of the activities listed above. It is going to be challenging. You are going to have to fight against your gut reactions that are connected to your hatred for the man who deceived you, but as you do this, you will discover that you are gaining control of the situation as well as yourself. You will have the ability to coax yourself into a condition of serenity, in which you will be able to exert self-control.

Imagine then that you come face to face with him. As you feel the old wrath building up inside you to such an intense degree that you worry you might erupt, you notice that your blood pressure is rising and that your heart is beating faster than usual. You decide to pause what you're doing rather than giving in to the wrath and the tension that are rapidly gaining control of your body. You temporarily cover your eyes with your hands. You inhale deeply, count to four, and then hold your breath for as long as you can. By doing this, you are not only calming yourself down but also blocking out the physical input that is making you angry. Your peripheral nervous system is stimulated whenever you take a breath in and then hold it for a period of time. Your heart receives a signal to slow down as a result of this. It is reading your lack of breathing as a need to conserve oxygen, which is done by beating less frequently. This is done because you have stopped breathing. It slows down because the more it beats, the more oxygen it needs, so the cycle continues. It is sufficient on its own to have a relaxing effect. After that, you can work on releasing the tension in your shoulders by starting to shrug them. You should take a few slow, deep breaths and try to relax even more. In the end, you will feel that rage melting away little by little, leaving behind your relaxed condition that is ready to confront your spouse without anger or rage. This state will allow you to face your spouse without anger or rage.

Altering your emotions can be done in a number of different ways; however, the most common technique is to transition from a state of agitation, anxiety, or grief into a state of calm and levelheadedness. This provides you with the opportunity to further evaluate your situation and surroundings in order to act in a manner that is acceptable. By harnessing the endorphins produced during exercise, you can induce feelings of joy or contentment in yourself. You can also induce patience by controlling your breathing and your body language.

www.ingramcontent.com/pod-product-compliance
Lightning Source LLC
Chambersburg PA
CBHW050255120526
44590CB00016B/2360